BEING HAUNTED

JENNIFER COPLEY

Cinnamon Press
:: small miracles from distinctive voices ::

Published by Cinnamon Press
Meirion House
Tanygrisiau
Blaenau Ffestiniog
Gwynedd, LL41 3SU
www.cinnamonpress.com

The right of Jennifer Copley to be identified as author of this work has been asserted by her in accordance with the Copyright, Designs and Patent Act, 1988. Copyright © 2019 Jennifer Copley.
ISBN: 978-1-78864-061-9
British Library Cataloguing in Publication Data. A CIP record for this book can be obtained from the British Library.
Designed and typeset in Palatino by Cinnamon Press.
Cover design by Jan Fortune. Printed in Poland
Cinnamon Press is represented in the UK by Inpress Ltd and in Wales by the Welsh Books Council

Acknowledgements

'When a Voice Moved Upon the Waters' was Commended in the Edwin Morgan Poetry Competition 2012
'Being Haunted' was Shortlisted in the Strokestown International Poetry Competition 2013
'On Shyness' won 2nd Prize in the Academi Cardiff International Poetry Competition 2007
'My Mother as a Curlew' was published in the 'Curlew Calling Anthology' 2017
'Just For Today' was Commended in the Troubadour Poetry Competition 2011

Contents

For Emily and Grace

Being Haunted

When a voice moved upon the waters

all the drowned, knowing it was their time,
kicked up from the ocean floor through mermaids
and shoals of fish, till they reached forgotten air.
Gathering themselves into groups
they struck out for dry land:
the blind towed by the un-blind, the limbless
clinging with their teeth to the ones in front,
bones being pushed ahead by bones.
It was dawn when they reached the shore,
shook salt from their hair, made fires,
dried those who could not help themselves.
And I saw my cousin and my aunt,
and I saw Icarus, heat steaming from his feathers,
and I saw my husband, still young, flicking water from his lashes
but I turned away so he would not find me.

Being Haunted

How annoying the dead are.
They breathe noisily
behind the curtains or crouch
under the table while we eat.
The dog watches all their to-ings and fro-ings.
He's never seen so many bones.

How boastful the dead are.
They can recite all the countries on the globe,
quote extensively from Keats or Kipling.
They know every fact about Mary Queen of Scots,
how she knelt to the axe,
her shivering dog under her skirts.

How spiteful the dead are.
Used to wintry weather, they relish it,
lash out at the postman blowing on his hands,
refuse to oil the gate.
They push the dog outside
and help themselves to his meat.

How scatterbrained the dead are.
We are forever picking up their stuff: spectacles,
the tea strainer, a small black paring knife.
The garden is littered with obituary notices.
Have a heart, we say, trying to rake the lawn
but only the dog reads our lips.

How nosy the dead are.
They peer round the wardrobe
as we lie in bed. They watch us sleep.
One of them goes through our In Box
to find out what we've ordered for Christmas –
handcuffs, racy underwear, a chewy slipper.

How determined the dead are.
When the dog dies, they wait and wait
for us to follow suit and when we do,
give us ice-cold tea so we never warm up.
They show us photos of God so we know what he looks like
but they won't tell us what to say.

On Shyness

My mother was shy,
my father was shy,
I am shy.
Everywhere I look for shyness.
I catch it in the flick-fin eyes of fishermen
or the lowered gaze of mariners
who run away to sea to be shy because
the sea, though you would not know it,
is very shy. Its waves hide behind each other
when bold feet come splashing.

The wind is shy but birds are not shy.
Brass-necked, they fly where they please
and the wind, being shy, has no idea
how to shoo them away.
On the whole, animals are not shy
with the exception of horses –
so insanely shy, they shy from everything.
Hiding inside their glossy coats,
forced over jumps and along busy roads,
all they want is to be back in their meadows.

I met an executioner once.
He was extremely shy.
He hid behind his black mask,
wore black gloves on his shy fingers,
whispered to me he was sorry
but he had a job to do.
In a little while, he said,
you will walk on the sea-shore
among the calm clear pebbles
which are the unshy eyes of the dead.

The Road to N.

The sky was white that day
and the sun was white.
There was no difference between them.
Don't look at the sun, they said,
it'll scar your eyes.

The field was white that day
and the horse was white.
Don't look at the horse, they said,
it doesn't belong there.
Look at the snow, how beautiful it is.

The road was white that day
and the house was white.
Don't look at the house, they said,
you don't live there anymore.
Look at the road. It goes to N.

I went to N.
Everything was black or grey.
I asked the people what they had lost.
Don't look at us, they said.

I found the church.
It had black pews and a black altar.
There was no priest
just a kohl-eyed woman
with wrinkled hands.

She showed me her polish and cloths,
the brasses of the dead.
There is no one here with that name, she said.

D(Owl)

Daughter of Owl
Goddess of Black
All day I lie hidden
At night I rise up
My eyes millwheels

My ancestor was Heaven-born
She pecked a hole in the sky to escape
I peck holes in the dead
Sometimes in the living

S(Cat)

Son of Cat
God of Black
All day I lie hidden
By night I curl from my cushion
Eyes pinion sharp

My ancestors were gods
They gave me claws
And pure sight

I(Tree)

Daughter of Tree & Sky
Gods of Light
By day I hide myself in leaves
By night I harbour
The fearful, the timorous

My husband Earth
Holds me strongly
To his warm self

(Woman)U

Granddaughter of Coasts & Seas
I can't hide my scaly skin, my fish eyes
What must I do?
I have no father
I have no mother
No one carries me

My Mother as a Curlew

The day I saw my mother as a curlew was a Wednesday,
the day the fish-man came.
It was raining. Her eyes were misty
with the worried look I remember.
She stared through the glass at me
and her wings beat fast to keep her in position.
The downward curve of her beak
was nothing like the snub she used to have
but her feathers were the colour of her hair when she was young.

Journey

I fell asleep with a journey in my hands.
I travelled down the blue line of a river
to the green woods.

It took many days to cross the moor,
avoid the lake
and climb the black mountain.

The map had many folds.
Each time I reached one I had to change direction.
The sea arrived too quickly.

There were plenty of places to get lost.
The white space round the edge was my mother's death.
The hard cover was my father's face.

I wanted to feel warm but ended up here—
blue icebergs, a silent shore.

The Mothers

The mothers are gone
and those who saw them leave
are gone.

The mothers carried handbags,
handbags that smelt of Coty powder
bought in Timothy Whites with old money

handbags with mints and bus tickets
caught in the linings,
handbags with small bone-handled knives
for eating apples in the park,
handbags with handkerchiefs.

We are heirs to those handbags.
They hold the dust of mothers.
Oh hold them close
Oh hold us all tight.

Three Pebbles

In my hand are three pebbles –
mother, father, daughter.
I carry them home in my pocket –
mother, father, daughter.
Which currents brought them here –
mother, father, daughter.
All their sins together –
mother, father, daughter.
Shaped and smoothed by ocean and by time –
mother, father, daughter.
Full of a great yearning –
mother, father, daughter.

Holiday etc.

He came back from the beach with a scallop shell,
stood back while she admired it.
The other day he'd bought her an expensive hat.
She felt obliged to wear it.

The sun beat down on their bodies
as they lay on the beach.
He went lobster red but refused cream
or later, calamine lotion.

The holiday was full of silences.
He stopped trying to speak French
after the implacable locals refused
to understand his request for a stamp.

They got home exhausted just as the man
from the kennels appeared to tell them
that their dog had died the day before.
Pancreatitis. There was nothing the vet could do.

The shock took all her strength. His blisters wept.
All night they sat by the blanket-full on the sofa
hoping it would move. But there was no mistake.
Next day he dug the hole. She held his coat.

Gone Wrong

It was words gone wrong
It was summer ice
It was words that lay by themselves
by the bare fire.

It was a cold wind
It was his words and hers
driven like dead leaves
along all the roads.

It was constant rain
It was spite and temper
It was words that fell without stopping
hitting the yard the clothes line the clothes.

It was a back street
It was a dog
nosing through rubbish
no home to go to.

It

Was it a Tom or a Harry who stole it?
Where did they hide it and why did they pawn it?

Who was the broker who kept it and cut it?
Trusted his wife with a razor to skin it?

How did the daughter wrap it and parcel it?
How did the granddaughter tuck in the ends of it?

Who was the postman who took and transported it?
Why did he sniff it and lick it and squeeze it?

How did it spring from its box and accuse him?
How many hours did it mock and abuse him?

Was it an eye or a lip or a finger?
Was it a lungful of ash or a cinder?

Was it a needle, an egg or a fish?
Was it a promise, a lie or a kiss?

Was it a soul just leaving a chest
Or was it one already at rest?

If I knew the answer, I'd never say.
I'd press my lips together, turn my face away.

The Unfulfilled

Why did nobody come? she asked her mother.
They had spent the morning in preparation
hoovering round the chairs and flapping a duster
across the mantelpiece.
She'd put on her blue dress with the white collar
and smart (but awkward) sleeves.
Her mother took out her hearing aid
and cleaned away the wax.
Lastly the door locks were greased
so they could be bolted once everyone was inside.
The windows were already securely nailed.

Key

The key I found in the drawer of your desk,
still with its label but the words washed out,
belongs to no door or cupboard in this house
and you are too long dead to tell me anything.

The Hollow Hill

When you lead me into the dark
I catch my breath at the cold
but, like the woodcutter's daughter,
who gave her heart to the squire's son,
I follow the sound of your steel-toed boots
in faith and trust.

When we get to the room you've prepared
with a fire and candles,
you remove your coat
and out of its pockets and sleeves
fly so many birds,
the cave roof blurs with blue and gold.

It's out of my hands what happens now.
My mother and father, the cushions, the clock,
the plates on the dresser—all their white white faces—
uselessly waiting for me to come back.

Island Woman

Why are you so thin, o island woman?
You can fit through a slit in the wall
as narrow as my toothbrush.
Your bones are sharp corners under your clothes,
they twist and they turn looking for a way out.
I wish you were not so thin.
You left the chicken on your plate last night
and just ate its neck which was very small.
I had chips but you had plain boiled rice
nibbled up with a spoon.

Why are you so tall, o island woman?
Everyone loves you yet you look as if
you're trying to get away, higher and higher,
your long neck searching the clouds.
I wish you were not so tall.
I want you to sit down so I can stop
tipping back my head to look in your eyes.
You put a slate back on the chimney
just by reaching up, I swear I saw you
though it was very dark, the moon a tiny
scratch of white on black.

Your Old Heart

When I came back I didn't understand what it looked like
Your heart all empty   nothing moving
I tried putting my lips to it but they were too cold

I know what I did to you
If I could undo it I would

And yet I like it here –
The blue sky and environs
The blue silk clothes all of us have to wear
We look alike and there's no shame

I think you will come to me soon
You don't need that old heart anyway

You can't buy sadness here
Which is good

Just For Today

they've come back, slipping between
the two tall trees at the garden's end.

No one gave them permission, they just came;
clean hands ready for tea, hair wet with summer rain.

And so she dries them slowly,
rubbing their heads gently with the blue beach towel.

She'll ask them to stay but they can't, they won't.
They'll be gone tomorrow

though she'll stand by the two tall trees,
look and look till it's too dark to see.

But for now she rubs their hair as slowly as she can
till they pull away, wanting their tea.

They have clean hands, they say, and lift them up.

www.ingramcontent.com/pod-product-compliance
Lightning Source LLC
Chambersburg PA
CBHW020449030426
42337CB00014B/1474